Moses Nsubuga Sekatawa

Moses Nsubuga Sekatawa

Have Some Money

Dedicated to

the congregation at Christ Reigns Worship Centre (Lower Konge, Kampala, Uganda). In appreciation of your prayers and Christian love. In Jesus' Name, I pray that you will continue to prosper and be in health even as your souls prosper to the glory of God, and your perfect joy. I pray that you will never lose the fear of God, the character of Christ, and the comfort of the Holy Ghost. May each of you spend all their days in prosperity and all their years in God-glorifying pleasures in the Name of our Lord Jesus Christ. Amen.

Scriptural quotations are all derived from the Authorized (King James) Version of the Bible unless otherwise specified.

Sometimes they have been interpreted or simply alluded to, to suit individual application. Translations and paraphrases are all by me.

Needless to say, the nouns and pronouns by which satan and his cohorts are addressed do not bear any capital letters in my books unless it is a printing error.

Yours in Christ,
Moses Nsubuga Sekatawa.

Have Some Money

Contents

Have Some Money

1.

Do you love MONEY?

Money is not evil. It is the love of money which is evil. I have seen money in the hands of the righteous. They use it to glorify God. To the wicked, money dictates terms. To the righteous, money obeys the counsel of God. It is a much better thing for the righteous to have some money than not to have any.

It pleases God to see His servants prosper.[1] Nevertheless, He is displeased when He sees us give His place in our lives to

---

[1] Psalm 35:27.

money or any other thing.[2]   When money takes the place of God in a person's life, the door is opened for endless sorrows to begin. Someone can be guilty of this sin when they have money or when they do not have it. It is a heart problem.

> 10.   For the love of money is the root of all evil: which while some coveted after, they have erred from the faith, and pierced themselves through with many sorrows.
>
> 11.   But thou, O man of God, flee these things; and follow after righteousness, godliness, faith, love, patience, meekness.
>
> 12.   Fight the good fight of faith, lay hold on eternal life, whereunto thou art also called, and hast professed a good profession before many witnesses.
>
> - 1 Timothy 6:10-12.

The love, and worship of money compromises a person's loyalty to God. You

---

[2] Exodus 20:2-5.

cannot serve two masters.[3]   That ungodly desire for wealth pierces a person's heart through with many sorrows.[4]

It is impossible to enjoy the peace of God while nursing and cherishing devilish ideas about money.

We should flee from the love of money.[5] We should follow after the righteousness of God, godliness, faith, love, patience, meekness and every other God glorifying virtue.[6] We should lay hold of eternal life[7] and never miss out on it. What a race! *"Flee..., follow after..., fight..., lay hold"*.[8]

There are some people who love money for money's sake. They are so materialistic that they can do anything to obtain it.[9] When they get money, it is used to gratify their carnal desires; to gorge their ungodly appetites. Their budgets can be split into three subtitles: the lust of the flesh, the lust of

---

[3] Matthew 6:24.
[4] 1 Timothy 6:10.
[5] 1 Timothy 6:10-11.
[6] 1 Timothy 6:11.
[7] 1 Timothy 6:12.
[8] 1 Timothy 6:11-12.
[9] James 4:2.

the eyes, and the pride of life.[10] Their god is their belly. Their end is destruction.

> 18. (For many walk, of whom I have told you often, and now tell you even weeping, *that they are* the enemies of the cross of Christ:

> 19. Whose   end *is* destruction, whose   God *is*   *their* belly, and *whose* glory *is* in their shame, who mind earthly things.)

> - Philippians 3:18-19.

Money can be a very dangerous master. Several people have taken lives of others so as to obtain some money. Countless suicides have resulted from money problems. The love of money has been responsible for many conflicts in society.

We have, millions of economists but the economic situation has been getting worse in almost every nation of the world! It is not uncommon to hear about treasurers or bank managers who took their lives, or were killed because of financial reasons.

We thank God for the great economic principles in the minds of people. There is still a very great need for the hearts to be equipped with holy knowledge concerning money.

There is a treasure greater than money. That treasure cost the life of Jesus Christ, the Son of the Living God. It is eternal life. Your soul is immortal. We will all live for ever but on different addresses. Some will live with Jesus[11] while others will spend a terrible eternity in the Lake of Fire.[12] Your soul is very important to God.

> 36. For what shall it profit a man, if he shall gain the whole world, and lose his own soul?
>
> 37. Or what shall a man give in exchange for his soul?
>
> - Mark 8:36-37.

---

[11] 1 Thessalonians 4:13-17; Revelation 21:1-7.
[12] Revelation 20:11-15 & 21:8.

Moses Nsubuga Sekatawa

Chapter

2.

Do you need MONEY?

There are people who need money. They desire to have it so they may meet their righteous budgets. There is nothing wrong with that.

There were people during Jesus' time on earth who used their resources to minister to Jesus and to promote His God ordained ministry.[1]

According to the Word of God there are

---

[1] Luke 8:1-3.

blessings for all those who obey Him.[2] We know that our Lord Jesus obeyed His Father in all things.[3] More to that, the Lord Jesus said; "All things that the Father hath are Mine"[4] Could He own everything that belongs to the Father and still be called poor? Emphatically, NO. He only became poor by choice, for our sake, when He became sin in our stead.[5] He became poor that we might become rich.

> 9. For ye know the grace of our Lord Jesus Christ, that, though he was rich, yet for your sakes he became poor, that ye through his poverty might be rich.
>
> 2 Corinthians 8:9

No doubt the Lord Jesus had personal needs while living on earth.[6] That does not mean our Lord Jesus lived a property stricken life full of lack as some people teach. Lack in the life and ministry of Jesus would have been

---

[2] Deuteronomy 28:1-14, Job 36:11 & Isaiah 1:19.
[3] Isaiah 55:11, Matthew 3:16-17 & 17:5.
[4] John 16:15.
[5] 2 Corinthians 5:21, 8:9.
[6] Matthew 4:2, 17:24-27, Luke 4:2, 9:58, 19:28-31, John 4:7, Hebrews 4:15,

a violation of the covenant on His Father's part. Yes, He obviously had needs but they were always met.[7]

Paul the apostle had to fulfill the calling of God upon his life. There were two ways he could do this after prayer. He had to come up with some godly income generating projects.

Paul the apostle was a tentmaker.[8] He engaged himself in some income generating projects so he would have a personal source of income lest he became a burden to anyone.[9] It was a very good thing for Paul to have a source of income. It saves a lot of pain when a servant of God has a personal source of income which does not tempt the servant of God to compromise his or her calling. For example a servant of God should not be a drug trafficker or the manager of a brothel.

He also expressed a need for his missions to be supported by the resources of God's people.[10] There is nothing wrong with a

[7] Psalm 84:11.
[8] Acts 18:1-3.
[9] Acts 20:33-34.
[10] 2 Corinthians 9:1-15, Philippians 4:10-19.

servant of God receiving donations to help accomplish a God-given assignment just as there is nothing wrong with anyone giving financial support to a servant of God to help them accomplish a God-given task.[11]

It is normal to need funds for a God glorifying project or for your godly personal budget. Needing money is far much different from loving money. Those who need money could live happily if there was another way for their needs to be met. The people who love money simply treat it as an object of worship. It is their idol. That is an abomination before God.[12]

The Lord Jesus said the Father will meet our needs so that our joy may be complete.[13] God will not withhold any good thing from those who walk uprightly.[14] He delights in meeting our needs. The apostle Paul told those Philippians who supported his ministry that God would meet all their needs.

19. But my God shall supply all

---

[11] Matthew 10:9-13, 40-42, 1 Timothy 5:17-18.
[12] Luke 16:13-15.
[13] John 16:23-24.
[14] Psalm 84:11.

your need according to his riches
in glory by Christ Jesus.

> - Philippians 4:19.

The Bible is full of scriptures which
encourage us not to worry about material
things because God is our provider.[15]

> 6. Be careful for nothing; but in
> every thing by prayer and
> supplication with thanksgiving let
> your requests be made known
> unto God.
>
> 7. And the peace of God, which
> passeth all understanding, shall
> keep your hearts and minds
> through Christ Jesus.

> - Philippians 4:6-7.

---

[15] Matthew 6:11, 25-33.

Moses Nsubuga Sekatawa

Chapter

3.

Do you want MONEY?

1.   The LORD *is* my   shepherd;   I shall not want.

2.   He maketh me to lie down in green   pastures: He   leadeth   me beside the still waters.

- Psalm 23:1-2.

There are some people who want money. They lack money. They need to engage in some gainful employment so they may have an   income   lest   their   lives   become   so miserable. Human needs are so real. You cannot afford to go through life depending on handouts from generous sympathizers.

Beloved, your Shepherd makes you to lie down in green pastures but He does not chew the grass for you. He leads you beside the still waters but He does not drink on your behalf. You have a great responsibility to make your God given opportunities worthwhile.

Prayer is very important. It has its place in our lives and ministries which nothing else can fill and nothing else should ever take. However, in addition to prayer we have to work. There are some things that prayer will not do. For instance the Lord Jesus raised Jairus' daughter from the dead and then tasked His audience to give her food.[1] Yes, prayer can bring the dead her back to life. However, hunger requires food. In order to have food you need a farmer, and some other marketplace people. So prayer should not be a substitute for work, just as work should never be a substitute for prayer.

---

[1] Mark 5:21-46.

It is selfish for any able person to evade work and then take advantage of those who labour.[2] It is also ungodly for someone to evade family responsibilities in the name of prayer, and ministry.[3]

There are some dear saints who waste their youthful years being idle. They say they cannot work because God called them to ministry. That is quite honourable if they would be busy for the Lord. The painful truth is that some of these professing 'full-time ministers' may spend a year or more without attempting to win a single soul for the Kingdom of God. If God has called you and set you apart as His minister then please do the work of an evangelist, make full proof of thy ministry.[4]

Work does not necessarily mean being employed by someone else. God will bless what you do because it is His will for your life. God does not call anyone to be idle but to serve Him. God's Word rebukes sluggards![5]

---

[2] 1 Thessalonians 3:10.
[3] 1 Timothy 5:8

[4] 2 Timothy 4:5.
[5] Proverbs 6:4-11.

God promises to bless the work of our hands.[6] Godly people should be the busiest because they are candidates for the blessings and favour of God. Everything a godly person does will prosper.[7] It is scripturally impossible to obey God and then live a life perpetually full lack[8] because God blesses obedience.[9] God is not idle. God works.[10] We should imitate God.[11]

> 10. For even when we were with you, this we commanded you, that if any would not work, neither should he eat.
>
> - 2 Thessalonians 3:10.

There are those who claim they used to be thieves and that is the only work they can do. So they would rather be idle than exercise their skill. It is good to know they have a sense of humour but they should still find some God glorifying, income generating work to do.

---

[6] Deuteronomy 28:12.
[7] Psalm 1:1-3.
[8] Job 36:11, Psalm 23:1, Psalm 34:10, Psalm 94:11
[9] Isaiah 1:19.
[10] John 5:17.
[11] Ephesians 5:1.

28. Let him that stole steal no more: but rather let him labour, working with *his* hands the thing which is good, that he may have to give to him that needeth.

- Ephesians 4:28.

Of course there are some others who fear to carry the cross. They dread ministry because they prefer the counsel of humanity to the wisdom and mercy of God. They prefer an earthly career to a heavenly calling. They become very busy in things contrary to God's will for their lives. God hates rebellion. When God employs you, that becomes your Number One office. Your God given assignment becomes the crusade of your life. Every other thing may be very good but it should come as Number Two after your obedience to God is fulfilled. If you sense the calling of God upon your life, you should seek to find out from God about His plans for you. If He has honoured you enough to speak to you about serving Him, you should have confidence in His love for you.

Ask Him about how your needs will always

be met. God speaks! He understands and speaks every language far much better than we can. He is the Author of every language.[12] He is more concerned about your life and family than you are.[13]

There is another problem of those who have never heard God speak to them about full time ministry, yet they delight in serving Him. Such people should serve God while doing their secular work as long as their secular responsibilities are not ungodly as far as the written Word of God is concerned. They are not rebellious. They are doing their best according to the revealed counsel of God for their lives.

Some people fear seeking God because they think whoever seeks Him ends up a preacher of the gospel. That is not true. There are some people who are not necessarily preachers but sought God to know His will for their lives. He gave them a business idea and hey became so prosperous. They use their wealth to help spread the gospel.

---

[12] Genesis 11:1-9.
[13] Matthew 6:25-33.

Having said that, what is wrong with proclaiming the good news of our resurrected Saviour who paid the supreme price for our redemption? Success is not necessarily a result of working hard. True success is the result of obeying God and doing His perfect will for your life.[14]

---

[14] Joshua 1:8, Job 36:11, Isaiah 48:17.

Chapter
4.

Does MONEY evade you?

There are some people in life who work so hard but never get anywhere close to success. They may have the best business plans and skills but their projects always abort at the eleventh hour. Success and victory are never close to them at all. Many of them are labouring under a curse.

The curse of poverty may be a result of unfaithfulness to God in financial matters. Sometimes it can be the result of some innocent human blood having been shed by that individual, or their ancestors. It may also be a result of someone rejecting the counsel of God for their lives! When a person rejects the counsel of God for their lives, they have to go on depending on their human strength. There are certain levels of victory to which our talents and skills can never carry us. We all need God!

Scriptural reasons why some people do not prosper:

1. Ignorance of God's Word concerning their lives:

Ignorance has never been a defense for any person against the devices of satan.[1] Neither has it ever been an opportunity for promotion in the Kingdom of God.[2] When a person lives a life contrary to the will of God for the lives, a door is opened for the enemy to take advantage of them.[3] God is not impressed by anyone's wilful rejection of the knowledge He has revealed.

> 6. My people are destroyed for lack of knowledge: because thou hast rejected knowledge, I will also reject thee, that thou shalt be no

---

[1] 2 Corinthians 2:11.
[2] Isaiah 5:13.
[3] 1 Samuel 15:23.

priest to Me: seeing thou hast forgotten the law of thy God, I will also forget thy children.

- Hosea 4:6.

2. **Rebellion against God.**

According to the Word of God, there is no difference between rebellion and witchcraft. God also sees no difference between stubbornness and iniquity or idolatry.

God told Saul to "go and smite Amalek, and utterly destroy all that they have, and spare them not; but slay both man and woman, infant and suckling, ox and sheep, camel and ass" – 1 Samuel 15:3. Saul's obedience to God in this matter was 99%.

> 7. And Saul smote the Amalekites from Havilah *until* thou comest to Shur, that *is* over against Egypt.
>
> 8. And he took Agag the king of the Amalekites alive, and utterly destroyed all the people with the edge of the sword.

9. But Saul and the people spared Agag, and the best of the sheep, and of the oxen, and of the fatlings, and the lambs, and all *that was* good, and would not utterly destroy them: but every thing *that was* vile and refuse, that they destroyed utterly.

- 1 Samuel 15:7-9.

There is no such a thing as obeying God 99%. It is either 100% obedience, or no obedience at all. Saul's rebellion caused him to lose the kingdom. He lost his God given position of authority and favour. God abhors rebellion.

22. And Samuel said, Hath the LORD *as great* delight in burnt offerings and sacrifices, as in obeying the voice of the LORD? Behold, to obey *is* better than sacrifice, *and* to hearken than the fat of rams.

23. For rebellion *is as* the sin of witchcraft, and stubbornness *is as* iniquity and idolatry. Because thou

hast rejected the word of the LORD, he hath also rejected thee from *being* king.

- 1 Samuel 15:22-23.

The italicized words were added by the translators for clarity. So you could as well remove them and just say, *"For rebellion the sin of witchcraft, and stubbornness iniquity and idolatry"*. That is why when a person rebels they come out of God's divine covering and end up with another master, satan.

It is unscriptural for God to bless and promote a person living in rebellion to His will.[4]

3. <u>Greed and lack of good stewardship:</u>

God's Word promises that He will supply all our need. He did not promise to supply all our greed.

Greed puts the flesh on the throne of our lives. It leads to poor stewardship of the treasures God has entrusted us with. The antidote for greed is generosity.[5]

---

[4] Deuteronomy 28:15-68, Proverbs 13:15, Isaiah 1:18-20, 59:1-2.
[5] Ephesians 4:28.

The Lord Jesus told a story of one young man who forsook the comfort of his father's home because of greed. He wandered in a strange land. His poor stewardship caused him to waste all "his substance with riotous living". He starved to an extent of desiring to fill his belly with the husks that the swine did eat.

11. And he said, A certain man had two sons:

12. And the younger of them said to *his* father, Father, give me the portion of goods that falleth *to me.* And he divided unto them *his* living.

13. And not many days after the younger son gathered all together, and took his journey into a far country, and there wasted his substance with riotous living.

14. And when he had spent all, there arose a mighty famine in that land; and he began to be in want.

15. And he went and joined himself to a citizen of that country;

and he sent him into his fields to feed swine.

16. And he would fain have filled his belly with the husks that the swine did eat: and no man gave unto him.

- Luke 16:11-16.

There are others who do not keep a record of their incomes and expenditures. Many times these unfaithful stewards spend their money unwisely not knowing the difference between their gross and net profit. We have always been told, *"A fool and his treasures are quickly parted"*. What a painful truth!

4. <u>The shedding of innocent human blood:</u>

When a person sheds innocent human blood, nature bears witness against him or her before God. That is what Cain experienced.[6] He became a stranger to the fellowship and blessings of God. His family owned the entire planet. He would till the ground and invest but would never know the joy of a harvest.

---

[6] Genesis 4:8-14.

8.   And Cain talked with Abel his brother: and it came to pass, when they were in the field, that Cain rose up against Abel his brother, and slew him.

9.   And the LORD said unto Cain, Where *is* Abel thy brother? And he said, I know not: *Am* I my brother's keeper?

10. And he said, What hast thou done? the voice of thy brother's blood crieth unto me from the ground.

11. And now *art* thou cursed from the earth, which hath opened her mouth to receive thy brother's blood from thy hand;

12. when thou tillest the ground, it shall not henceforth yield unto thee her strength; a fugitive and a vagabond shalt thou be in the earth.

13. And Cain said unto the LORD, My punishment *is* greater than I can bear.

14. Behold, thou hast driven me out this day from the face of the earth; and from thy face shall I be hid; and I shall be a fugitive and a vagabond in the earth; and it shall come to pass, *that* every one that findeth me shall slay me.

- Genesis 4:8-14.

There are some people who work so hard everyday. They may have the best business plans. They may have the best contacts in the land. They may even seem to have an advantage above the rest by virtue of their birth, profession, talents and skills. Yet they are strangers to success. Their output cannot justify the wisdom, time and resources they invested. Their lives are full of toil, sweat and tears of frustration. Many times they end up vagabonds *(Please get my book, "**Break the curses**")*.

5. <u>Concealing sin and pseudo-repentance.</u>

There is need to confess and forsake sin if a child of God has to prosper. Mere confession of sin, without a decision to forsake our wicked ways is no good and can never lead anyone closer to God. There are some people who confess their sins all the time, without their lives bearing any fruits to justify the words spoken while in prayer. That is pseudo-repentance. True repentance means changing one's thoughts and ways.[7]

> 13. He that covereth his sins shall not prosper: but whoso confesseth and forsaketh *them* shall have mercy.
>
> - Proverbs 28:13.

God is so much interested in the motives of our hearts.

> 18. If I regard iniquity in my heart, the Lord will not hear *me:*
>
> - Psalm 66:18.

6. Slothfulness:

Laziness leads to poverty. Slothfulness is even worse because it is the laziness of the heart. Someone does not work just because they are unwilling to work. They are sluggards.

---

[7] Isaiah 55:7

6.   Go to the ant, thou sluggard; consider her ways, and be wise:

7.   which having no guide, overseer, or ruler,

8.   provideth her meat in the summer, *and* gathereth her food in the harvest.

9.   How long wilt thou sleep, O sluggard? when wilt thou arise out of thy sleep?

10. *Yet* a little sleep, a little slumber, a little folding of the hands to sleep:

11. so shall thy poverty come as one that travelleth, and thy want as an armed man.

- Proverbs 6:6-11.

7. The snare of evil confessions:

Twelve Israelites were sent out on a spying mission. The land of Canaan belonged to them because God had given it to them. God intended them to possess the land. Ten of them chose to speak words contrary to the promise of God for their lives. They depended upon the counsel of their sight instead of God's Word.

They saw themselves as grasshoppers and saw their adversaries as great men. They missed the God given promise. They wandered in the wilderness for forty years without ever getting to their promised land.[8] Talk about motion without progress!

Words are so important. They are not play toys. They either shape a person's destiny or seal a person's fate.[9] You can make or lose friends and money just because of the words you choose to speak and believe.

Many people are poor and their businesses fail because they are ensnared by their evil words contrary to the promises of God. It is impossible for a person to rise above the meaning of their spoken words.

> 2. thou art snared with the words of thy mouth, thou art taken with the words of thy mouth.
>
> - Proverbs 6:2.

---

[8] Numbers 13 & 14.
[9] Matthew 12:37.

The power to destroy business ideas or to promote them is in the tongue. Great visions born in heaven have been destroyed by human tongues that emit negative energy.

> 21. Death and life *are* in the power of the tongue: and they that love it shall eat the fruit thereof.
>
> - Proverbs 18:21.

The Bible says, *"Money answereth all things"* – Ecclesiastes 10:19. If money answereth all things then money heareth all things. Money can flee from you or come your way depending on your confession. You cannot answer what you haven't heard. So what kind of words is your wealth prosperity listening to? Words are seeds.[10] The words your sow determine the harvest you receive.

8. <u>Fighting against God's servants:</u>

God's servants are agents of prosperity.[11] God is interested in the way we receive and treat His servants.[12] When a person demeans, ridicules, criticizes, curses or by

---

[10] Mark 4:14.
[11] 2 Chronicles 20:20.
[12] Matthew 10:40-42, John 13:20.

any means fights against any servant of God, that person becomes a candidate of God's wrath and a stranger to prosperity. No one ever prospers by becoming a weapon against God's anointed.

> 17. No weapon that is formed against thee shall prosper; and every tongue *that* shall rise against thee in judgment thou shalt condemn. This *is* the heritage of the servants of the LORD, and their righteousness *is* of Me, saith the LORD.
>
> - Isaiah 54:17.

5.

Have some MONEY.

There Word of God spells His will out for His children. God delights in the prosperity of His servants.[1]

> 2. Beloved, I wish above all things that thou mayest prosper and be in health, even as thy soul prospereth.
>
> 3. For I rejoiced greatly, when the brethren came and testified of the truth that is in thee, even as thou walkest in the truth.

---

[1] Psalm 35:27.

4.   I have no greater joy than to hear that my children walk in truth.

- 2 John 2-4.

Walking in the truth includes an element of honesty and sincerity but it also means having the correct information and living by it, while we allow our steps to be ordered by God accordingly. God is so concerned about our prosperity that He put principles of success for us in His Word. I would like to share some twelve principles of prosperity with you.

1.   <u>Walking with God.</u>

Joseph was sold to slavery in Egypt yet there was a seed of prosperity in his life because he lived a life pleasant to God. It may not matter what society does to you, or calls you as long as your lifestyle wins the smile of Jesus.

> 1.   And Joseph was brought down to Egypt; and Potiphar, an officer of Pharaoh, captain of the guard, an Egyptian, bought him of the hands of the Ishmeelites, which had brought him down thither.

2. And the LORD was with Joseph, and he was a prosperous man; and he was in the house of his master the Egyptian.

3. And his master saw that the LORD *was* with him, and that the LORD made all that he did to prosper in his hand.

- Genesis 39:1-3.

Joseph was never affected by the historical, geographical, or economic factors of his environment. Even the prison was not strong enough to affect his God-given favour and prosperity. It was his relationship with God which always mattered.

21. But the LORD was with Joseph, and shewed him mercy, and gave him favour in the sight of the keeper of the prison.

22. And the keeper of the prison committed to Joseph's hand all the prisoners that *were* in the prison; and whatsoever they did there, he was the doer *of it*.

23. The keeper of the prison looked not to any thing *that was* under his hand; because the LORD was with him, and *that* which he did, the LORD made *it* to prosper .

- Genesis 39:21-23.

2.   Obedience to God:

Obedience to God means nothing less than our absolute surrender to Him. Obedience is the highest sacrifice because it is a sacrifice of one's will. Just like the Lord Jesus in the Garden of Gethsemane, someone has a will yet they say to the Lord, "Not my will, but thine, be done"[2]. Obedience starts where agreement stops. God rewards obedience with blessings.[3]

We need to remember that *"The blessing of the LORD, it maketh rich, and He addeth no sorrow with it"* – Proverbs 10:22. True prosperity therefore goes beyond the possession of material things. It includes righteousness, peace and joy in the Holy

---

[2] Luke 22:42

[3] Deuteronomy 28:1-14, 1 Chronicles 22:13.

Ghost. True prosperity is for those who choose to obey God and do His will.

> 11. If they obey and serve *Him*, they shall spend their days in prosperity, and their years in pleasures.
>
> - Job 36:11.

3.   Faith in God and in His counsel.

Faith in God establishes us. Faith in His counsel causes us to prosper.[4]

It was an ugly moment when the nation of Israel was invaded by three mighty armies. They prayed and fasted. God gave them a word for their breakthrough. They were to go to the frontline with music and dancing. All they needed was faith in God and in the word spoken by His servants.

> 20. And they rose early in the morning, and went forth into the wilderness of Tekoa: and as they went forth, Jehoshaphat stood and said, Hear me, O Judah, and ye inhabitants of Jerusalem; Believe

---

[4] 2 Chronicles 20:20, Nehemiah 2:20.

in the LORD your God, so shall ye be established; believe his prophets, so shall ye prosper.

- 2 Chronicles 20:20.

A barren woman gave birth to Samuel who grew to be a mighty servant of God just because she believed in the word spoken by Eli the priest of her time.[5]

A group of experienced fishermen spent a fruitless night trying to catch fish. They toiled all night long but all their attempts were pathetic until the Lord Jesus gave them instructions. Their success was encapsulated in His words.

> 4. Now when he had left speaking, he said unto Simon, Launch out into the deep, and let down your nets for a draught.

> 5. And Simon answering said unto him, Master, we have toiled all the night, and have taken nothing: nevertheless at Thy word I will let down the net.

---

[5] 1 Samuel 1:1-20.

6. And when they had this done, they inclosed a great multitude of fishes: and their net brake.

7. And they beckoned unto *their* partners, which were in the other ship, that they should come and help them. And they came, and filled both the ships, so that they began to sink.

8. When Simon Peter saw *it*, he fell down at Jesus' knees, saying, Depart from me; for I am a sinful man, O Lord.

9. For he was astonished, and all that were with him, at the draught of the fishes which they had taken:

- Luke 5:4-9.

4. Thinking holy thoughts.

As a person thinks *(believes, expects, intends, remembers or is opinionated)* in his heart *(subconscious mind)*, so is he.[6] The

---

[6] Proverbs 23:7.

Lord Jesus said, "*Out of the abundance of the heart the mouth speaketh*" – Matthew 12:34.

One man said, "Watch your thoughts, they become your words; watch your words, they become your actions; watch your actions, they become your habits; watch your habits, they become your character; watch your character, it becomes your destiny." No wonder words from a heart full of righteousness, peace and joy of the Holy Ghost charge the atmosphere with God's presence. It all begins with the mind. What we fill our minds with determines the words we speak, the, actions we take, our habits, our character and finally our destiny.

We are encouraged to think holy thoughts. The easiest way to tame your mind and think holy thoughts is by meditating in the Word of God. The Psalmist said his armor against sin was the Word of God resident in him.[7]

We also learn the importance of meditating upon God's Word when we see the emphasis God laid on it while giving leadership instructions to Joshua after the death of Moses.

---

[7] Psalm 119:11.

8.   This book of the law shall not depart out of thy mouth; but thou shalt meditate therein day and night, that thou mayest observe to do according to all that is written therein: for then thou shalt make thy way prosperous, and then thou shalt have good success

- Joshua 1:8.

Meditating "therein day and night" in the Word of God is a prerequisite for success. God's concept of prosperity includes a prosperous soul. Your soul is your mind, intellect, emotions and will. God delights in seeing a mind renewed by His incorruptible Word.

2.   Beloved, I wish above all things that thou mayest prosper and be in health, even as thy soul prospereth.

- 2 John 2.

God is not against you possessing wealth. He is against wealth possessing you.

36. For what shall it profit a man, if he shall gain the whole world, and lose his own soul?

37. Or what shall a man give in exchange for his soul?

- Mark 8:36-37.

5.   <u>Speaking words of victory.</u>

As mentioned earlier on, it is impossible for anyone to rise above the level of their confession.

21. Death   and   life *are* in   the power of the tongue: and they that love it shall eat the fruit thereof.

- Proverbs 18:21.

23. For verily I say unto you, That whosoever shall say unto this mountain, Be thou removed, and be thou cast into the sea; and shall not doubt in his heart, but shall believe that those things which he saith shall come to pass; he shall have whatsoever he saith.

- Mark 11:23.

So much emphasis is put on what we say, *"Whosever shall say ... those things he saith ... shall have whatsoever he saith"* - Mark 11:23. We need to hold fast our confession of what the Word of God says about us because He Who promised is faithful.[8]

No one ever prospers by speaking curse words about their financial investments. We should always declare good things about our lives and businesses in Jesus' Name:

> 28. Thou shalt also decree a thing, and it shall be established unto thee: and the light shall shine upon thy ways.
>
> - Job 22:28.

I encourage you to read my book, "**Now faith is**".

6. <u>Seeking God.</u>

There is a very big difference between seeking God and seeking the things of God. *"For He that cometh to God must believe that He is"* – Hebrews 11:6. We come to God

---

[8] Hebrews 10:23

because He is. We do not come to God because He has.

It grieves the heart of God when His children long more for what He has, instead of Who and What He is. It is in seeking God that we find the fullness of joy resident in His presence.[9]

There is an anointing for prosperity that comes upon those who seek the Lord with all their hearts.

> 3. Sixteen years old *was* Uzziah when he began to reign, and he reigned fifty and two years in Jerusalem. His mother's name also *was* Jecoliah of Jerusalem.
>
> 4. And he did *that which was* right in the sight of the LORD, according to all that his father Amaziah did.
>
> 5. And he sought God in the days of Zechariah, who had understanding in the visions of God: and as long as he sought

---

[9] Psalm 16:11.

the LORD, God made him to prosper.

- 2 Chronicles 26:3-5.

7. Being aggressive against satanic forces:

Beloved, we have not been called to compromise with satan, or his cohorts. he is a thief who comes only to steal, to kill and to destroy.[10] he hates you. he hates your positive progress. he hates everything about you. he even hates those who submit to him. Given chance he would use anything against you, or your loved ones.[11] The Word of God instructs us not to allow satan any place in our lives.[12] The whole armor of God given us is not a preparation for a picnic.[13] We have been called to war,[14] and victory is our birthright.[15]

11. Lest Satan should get an advantage of us: for we are not

---

[10] John 10:10
[11] Job 1 & 2.
[12] Ephesians 4:27.
[13] Ephesians 6:10-18.
[14] 2 Corinthians 10:3-6, 2 Timothy 2:3-4.
[15] Isaiah 54:17, 1 John 5:4-5.

ignorant of his devices.

                                    - 2 Chronicles 26:3-5.

The Lord Jesus defeated satan for us at Calvary.[16] Our responsibility is to enforce and maintain what He did for us.[17] There is need for us to keep the enemy on the run by resisting him all the time.

> 7. Submit yourselves therefore to God. Resist the devil, and he will flee from you.
>
>   - James 4:7.

8. <u>Hard work:</u>

God is not lazy. The Lord Jesus said God works.[18] We have been called to be imitators of God.[19] It is God's will for us to be strong, and to work.

> 4. Yet now be strong, O Zerubbabel, saith the LORD; and be strong, O Joshua, son of Josedech, the high priest; and be

---

[16] Colossians 2:15, Hebrews 2:14.
[17] Matthew 28:18-20, Mark 16:15-18, John 14:12, Ephesians 5:1
[18] John 5:17.
[19] Ephesians 5:1.

> strong, all ye people of the land, saith the LORD, and work: for I *am* with you, saith the LORD of hosts:

> - Haggai 2:4.

God's Word encourages us to be very diligent and hardworking.

> 29. Seest thou a man diligent in his business? he shall stand before kings; he shall not stand before mean *men*.

> - Proverbs 22:29.

We are told not to be *"slothful in business"* – Romans 12:11.

9. <u>Hospitality and kindness to God's people:</u>

God loves people.[20] We were created in His image and in His likeness.[21] Evolution is as unscriptural as it is unscientific.

A story is told of a mother who always told her children that the human race was created

---

[20] John 3:16.
[21] Genesis 1:26-27, Ezekiel 1:26, James 3:9

by God in His image. The father always told them that people evolved from and apes. Desperate for the truth the children waited for dinner time and asked, *"Mummy, you say we were created by God in His image. Daddy says we evolved from apes. Who is right?"* The mother smiled and gave her answer. *"Both of us are right",* she said. *"I have told you where I came from. Daddy also told you his ancestry. I cannot really argue with him because I never saw his grandparents".*

Beloved, we were made in the image of God. When you are kind to God's people, He rewards your kindness with blessings.[22] When you show kindness to the poor, God pays you back.[23] According to the Word of God, a positive attitude towards Israel facilitates one's prosperity.[24]

When you give to God's anointed servants, you reap His blessing which makes rich and to which He adds no sorrow.[25] God's servants are agents of prosperity.[26]

---

[22] Ephesians 6:8.
[23] Proverbs 19:17
[24] Genesis 12:1-3, Psalm 122:6
[25] Proverbs 10:22.
[26] Genesis 12:1-2, Matthew 10:40-42.

40. He that receiveth you receiveth me, and he that receiveth me receiveth him that sent me.

41. He that receiveth a prophet in the name of a prophet shall receive a prophet's reward; and he that receiveth a righteous man in the name of a righteous man shall receive a righteous man's reward.

42. And whosoever shall give to drink unto one of these little ones a cup of cold *water* only in the name of a disciple, verily I say unto you, he shall in no wise lose his reward.

- Matthew 10:40-42.

10.   <u>Generosity.</u>

God is a generous God.[27]   He blesses us so that we may be a blessing to others. We are told to imitate God.[28]

It is also true that God rarely blesses individuals. Whatever He gives you cannot be

---

[27] Psalm 66:19, John 3:16, Ephesians 1:3 & 2 Peter 1:3.
[28] Ephesians 5:1.

intended to end with you. God blesses you so
hat others may benefit as well. For instance
why would He give Abraham the whole land of
Canaan at that old age?

1. Now the LORD had said unto
Abram, Get thee out of thy
country, and from thy kindred, and
from thy father's house, unto a
land that I will shew thee:

2. and I will make of thee a great
nation, and I will bless thee, and
make thy name great; and thou
shalt be a blessing:

3. and I will bless them that
bless thee, and curse him that
curseth thee: and in thee shall all
families of the earth be blessed.

- Genesis 12:1-3.

Abraham was blessed so that He too
would in turn be a blessing, and a channel of
God's blessings to all the families of the earth.

Generosity glorifies God causing joy
among His people.[29] Giving conquers the

---

[29] 2 Corinthians 9:6-9

greed in our hearts. God has never called anyone to be mean and stingy. Generosity is a key to prosperity.[30]

> 38. Give, and it shall be given unto you; good measure, pressed down, and shaken together, and running over, shall men give into your bosom. For with the same measure that ye mete withal it shall be measured to you again.
>
> - Luke 6:38.

11.   Tithes and offerings:

God was so concerned about the prosperity of His covenant people that He reminded them about His covenant principles of success. As far as their blessings were concerned, obedience to God was a prerequisite.

> 8.   Will a man rob God? Yet ye have robbed me. But ye say, Wherein have we robbed thee? In tithes and offerings.

---

[30] Proverbs 11:24-26.

9.   Ye *are* cursed with a curse: for ye have robbed me, *even* this whole nation.

10.   Bring ye all the tithes into the storehouse, that there may be meat in mine house, and prove me now herewith, saith the LORD of hosts, if I will not open you the windows of heaven, and pour you out a blessing, that *there shall* not *be room* enough *to receive it*.

11.   And I will rebuke the devourer for your sakes, and he shall not destroy the fruits of your ground; neither shall your vine cast her fruit before the time in the field, saith the LORD of hosts.

12.   And all nations shall call you blessed: for ye shall be a delightsome land, saith the LORD of hosts.

- Malachi 3:8-12.

The covenant was to the effect that they would give 10% of their increase back to God and they would bring offerings to the house of

God whenever they came to worship. It was an act of rebellion to go before the LORD empty handed.[31]

There are some dear saints of God who are deceived into thinking that the tithe was part of the law and as such we do not have to pay our tithes again. That is an item from satan's agenda to keep you in rebellion against God so that you may not enjoy the covenant blessings and protection of God.

The tithe started long before the law was introduced.[32] The Lord Jesus told the Pharisees to teach the whole counsel of God, including paying tithes.[33] The Bible says that even now we still pay our tithes.[34] I encourage you to get my book, *"Worshipping God with our resources"*.

Of course God in His sovereignty can bless any person but it is practically impossible to rob God then expect to enjoy His covenant blessings.[35]

---

[31] Exodus 23:15, 34:20.
[32] Genesis 14:18-20, 28:20-22.
[33] Matthew 23:23,
[34] Hebrews 7:8.
[35] Galatians 6:7.

12.   <u>Giving to the work of God:</u>

God's purpose for blessing us is not for us to be independent of Him.[36] Our comfort is so important. Comfort has its place in our lives which should not be underestimated. However, God is more interested in our character than in our comfort.[37]

Money should be a servant and never a master.[38] What is the eternal purpose for money if we cannot use it to serve God here on earth?[39]

It is quite wonderful to quote Philippians 4:19 and to encourage ourselves that God will meet all our needs. The trouble is that many dear saints of God quote that scripture out of context. They forget the way the verse begins. It begins with a conjunction; **"BUT"**. That should sober us up to realize the verse does not stand alone. It is a continuation of another statement.

19. But my God shall supply all your need according to His riches

---

[36] Deuteronomy 8:18
[37] Haggai 1:2-11
[38] Matthew 19:16-22, 1 Timothy 6:5-10.
[39] Exodus 25:1-2, 8.

in glory by Christ Jesus.

- Philippians 4:19.

A careful study of that whole fourth chapter of the epistle to the Philippians confirms to us the truth that Paul the apostle was addressing those saints who gave to the work God had called him to do. They supported his ministry with their resources. The promise, therefore is conditional. It is meant to be enjoyed by those who use their resources to support God's work.

> 9. Honour the LORD with thy substance, and with the firstfruits of all thine increase:
>
> 10. so shall thy barns be filled with plenty, and thy presses shall burst out with new wine.
>
> -Proverbs 3:9-10.

Even after the material blessings, God should remain in His place of Lordship over our lives. We have been called to serve God alone.[40] He is our Everlasting Father. He is

---

[40] Matthew 6:24.

the Fountain of living waters.[41] His counsel to us is still the same. Our intimacy with God should never be compromised.

God warned the children of Israel against forgetting Him after obtaining wealth. We too need to take that same warning very seriously.

> 10. When thou hast eaten and art full, then thou shalt bless the LORD thy God for the good land which He hath given thee.

> 11. Beware that thou forget not the LORD thy God, in not keeping His commandments, and his judgments, and His statutes, which I command thee this day:

> 12. lest *when* thou hast eaten and art full, and hast built goodly houses, and dwelt *therein;*

> 13. and *when* thy herds and thy flocks multiply, and thy silver and thy gold is multiplied, and all that thou hast is multiplied;

---

[41] Jeremiah 2:13.

14. then thine heart be lifted up, and thou forget the LORD thy God, which brought thee forth out of the land of Egypt, from the house of bondage;

15. Who led thee through that great and terrible wilderness, *wherein were* fiery serpents, and scorpions, and drought, where *there was* no water; Who brought thee forth water out of the rock of flint;

16. Who fed thee in the wilderness with manna, which thy fathers knew not, that He might humble thee, and that He might prove thee, to do thee good at thy latter end;

17. and thou say in thine heart, My power and the might of *mine* hand hath gotten me this wealth.

18. But thou shalt remember the LORD thy God: for *it is* He that giveth thee power to get wealth, that He may establish His covenant which He sware unto thy

fathers, as *it is* this day.
- Deuteronomy 8:10-18.

=========================

Beloved, Eternal life belongs to you because Jesus Christ the Son of the Living God paid the supreme price for your redemption.

We have all sinned and come short of the glory of God.[42] Spiritual death reigned in our lives because of sin. For the wages of sin is death.[43] God declared, *"The soul that sinneth, it shall die."*[44]

"But God commendeth his love toward us, in that, while we were yet sinners, Christ died for us" – Romans 5:8. Jesus Christ, the Son of the Living God, absolutely without sin, came on the scene and took our place in the courtroom of God's justice. Our guilt and its penalty were laid on Him.

---

[42] Romans 3:23, Isaiah 53:6.
[43] Romans 6:23.
[44] Ezekiel 18:4, 20.

4. Surely He hath borne our griefs, and carried our sorrows: yet we did esteem Him stricken, smitten of God, and afflicted.

5. But He *was* wounded for our transgressions, He *was* bruised for our iniquities: the chastisement of our peace *was* upon Him; and with His stripes we are healed.

6. All we like sheep have gone astray; we have turned every one to his own way; and the LORD hath laid on Him the iniquity of us all.

- Isaiah 53:4-6.

Jesus tasted death *(died and went to hell)* for every person.[45] He was raised from the dead by the Spirit of God[46] after He paid the Supreme price for our redemption. He was delivered on the account of our transgressions and was raised from the dead when we stood justified before God.[47] He defeated death, hell and the grave.[48] He broke the curse of sin

---

[45] Hebrews 2:9, 1 Peter 3:18.
[46] Romans 6:4.
[47] Romans 4:25.
[48] Hebrews 2:14, 1 Corinthians 15:51-57, Revelation 1:18.

over us.[49]   Right now, He is seated on the Father's right hand.[50]   He is interceding for us.[51]

Any person who comes to God through Jesus Christ is forgiven because the penalty for our transgressions was laid upon Jesus Christ. When judged in Christ, you cannot be found guilty. God the Supreme Judge then declares:

> 1.   *There is* therefore now no condemnation to them which are in Christ Jesus, who walk not after the flesh, but after the Spirit.
>
> - Romans 8:1.

Our debt was paid. No debt can legally be paid twice!

We do not have a sin problem any longer. All we have is the sinners' problem. It can be solved. Your sins can be remitted. If you would like to your sins to be forgiven you can. Please pray this prayer out loudly and clearly from the bottom of your heart:

---

[49] Galatians 3:13-14.
[50] Hebrews 1:3.
[51] Hebrews 7:25.

Dear Lord God,

I acknowledge that I am a sinner, unworthy of your love, fellowship and promises.

I know that Your Son, Jesus Christ died for my sins and was raised from the dead for my justification. I know that He is in heaven, seated on Your right hand.

Have mercy upon me. Please forgive me.

I do now receive and confess Your Son Jesus Christ as my Lord and Saviour.

Father, thank You so much for my salvation. In the Name of Jesus Christ, Amen.

If you have made a decision to commit your life to the Lordship of Jesus Christ, it will be important for you to belong to a Bible believing Church whose leaders are subject to the written Word of God. They will baptize you by immersion. They will teach you the Word of God. They will pray for you to be filled with the Holy Spirit. Now you are a believer.

The inward evidence to the believer of his salvation, is the direct witness of the Holy Spirit.[52] The outward evidence to all men is a life of righteousness and true holiness. This kind of life rejects such behaviour as homosexuality, lesbianism, sexual immorality and every form of sexual perversion, lust, incest, idolatry, envy, murder, strife, drunkenness, deceit, malice, gossip, slander, insolence, arrogance, boasting, promoting evil deeds, disobedience, greed, covetousness and all forms of moral depravity.[53]

You will need to bear fruit.

> 22. But the fruit of the Spirit is love, joy, peace, longsuffering, gentleness, goodness, faith,
>
> 23. meekness,   temperance: against such there is no law.
>
> - Galatians 5:22-23.

I pray that you will have a wonderful time

---

[52] Romans 8:16.
[53] Romans 1:18-32, Colossians 3:5.

living a life of obedience to God. In case we do not meet here on earth, we will meet along the golden streets and we will for ever rejoice in the presence of our Eternal Father. God bless you.

In case this book has been a blessing to you, please write a good review about it on www.amazon.com so that others may be encouraged to read it as well.

Your brother in Christ,

Moses Nsubuga Sekatawa.

Other books by Moses Nsubuga Sekatawa:

1. Spiritual female problems.
2. Now faith is.
3. Worshipping God with our resources.
4. Break the curses.
5. The Blood that speaketh better things.
6. Demolishing evil foundations.

Moses Nsubuga Sekatawa's books are available on www.amazon.com

Made in the USA
Columbia, SC
18 September 2022